Occasional Prayers
for the School Year

Gráinne Delaney

Published by Messenger Publications, 2022

ISBN 9781788125703

Designed by Messenger Publications Design Department
Front cover image © 2020 Irishasel/Shutterstock
Back cover adapted from Beatitudes for the Adolescent, Catholic Schools Week 2016
Back cover Beatitudes composed by students from Crescent College Comprehensive
Illustrations © Orla Delaney
Typeset in Academy Engraved, Adobe Garamond Pro, Adobe Caslon Pro,
Printed by Hussar Books

Messenger Publications,
37 Leeson Place, Dublin D02 E5V0
www.messenger.ie

This book can serve as a 'go-to' for anyone leading prayer in an environment that pays attention to the academic year in a liturgical, seasonal and thematic way.

These prayers, written and compiled by Gráinne Delaney, will most frequently be used at Friday Morning Prayer in Crescent College Comprehensive SJ, so if you pray these prayers, you join this weekly praying community. Each morning the community prays the prayer of St Ignatius. You are welcome to join. The prayer of St Ignatius can be found on page 70.

Gráinne Delaney is from Dundalk and was educated in St Vincent's Secondary School and Mater Dei Institute of Education. It was her role as chaplain at Crescent College Comprehensive SJ that developed her emphasis on faith formation.

Prayer is listening to the word of God expressed
through the circumstances of life;
God's word of comfort accompanying us through the joys and sorrows,
the shadows and darkness
as we make our way into the light.

JIM MAHER SJ

CONTENTS

DECEMBER

JANUARY

FEBRUARY

MARCH

APRIL

MAY

JUNE

JULY

AUGUST

Prayers and Reflections For
Any Time in the School Year

INTRODUCTION

Having worked for over twenty years in a Jesuit school where school gatherings are always prefaced with prayer, I often searched for and wrote different prayers to suit the school year, to suit a moment in time. Sometimes I had time to prepare; at other times I ran along corridors to pull something from my files or turned to the Internet while the bell was ringing and the whole school community was gathering. I often thought, 'I should have a book under my arm and trust that I will always have something to suit'. So I put my prayers together. I begin with this one, which I wrote while trying to incorporate the characteristics of Jesuit education, that is, that which has fed my heart for the past twenty years.

Lord God, you are always with us; we find you in all things. Help us as we begin a new year together, to act *in cura personalis*, care of the individual, in care of each other. During the coming months, may we use the gifts you have given us and so continue to grow towards freedom and responsibility to reach our full potential, to strive for excellence. May our learning reach out to those less fortunate than ourselves in the programmes and events in our school, so that our faith displays justice. May we, as an entire community, teach and learn in the year ahead. Give us confidence in our own openness and adaptability, so that we do not miss the opportunity to do things that we've never tried before. We make our prayer, in service of the Church and its mission and through Christ, the model for human life. Amen.

SEPTEMBER

Opening of the School Year

We gather as a school community, together again, giving thanks for the blessings we received during our summer holidays and to ask the Lord's continued blessing on this new school year. We welcome all our new pupils and staff and look forward to working as a community with you. We pray today for ourselves and each other, that we may support and help each other in the months ahead, so that we strive to be the best that we can be. Amen.

Jesus, I feel within me a great desire to please you but, at the same time, I feel totally incapable of doing this without your special light and help, which I can expect only from you. Accomplish your will within me – even in spite of me.

ST CLAUDE LA COLOMBIÈRE SJ
(*Hearts on Fire: Praying with Jesuits*, Michael Harter SJ)

SEPTEMBER

Working Together

What will this year bring? You do not know; I do not know.

It will bring its usual quota of work and play, of success and failure, all the things that are part of school life.

It is a new beginning, the planting of a seed that will grow for a year, the seed of fruit that will blossom in times to come.

It is a new hope, hope for good work, for successful results, for friendship, for fun, for learning.

May there be hard work, faith and friendship.

May we, this year, together act justly,

together love tenderly,

and together walk humbly with our God. Amen.

Now there are varieties of gifts, but the same Spirit; and there are varieties of services, but the same Lord; and there are varieties of activities, but it is the same God who activates all of them in everyone. To each is given the manifestation of the Spirit for the common good.

1 CORINTHIANS 12:4–7

SEPTEMBER

Blessings on All

Blessed are you
who walks in step, inside the school gate

or stands to watch as others march and join in once again
or sit in the company of others, embraced as friends
and feel excited or delighted to be back in the hands of the school.

Lord, let us pause to imagine the day and year ahead.

Let's reflect on the wonder of what might happen and what we together might
make happen.

Morning will come and evening will come each day; help us to trust that there
is nothing that we can't handle together.

Bless each person planted here, each one making this school happen,
and as the seasons turn, we will have seasons too.

No one will stand still, we will all grow, all share, all leaves will change.

Journey with us this year. Amen.

Faithful friends are a sturdy shelter:
whoever finds one has found a treasure.
Faithful friends are beyond price;
no amount can balance their worth.
Faithful friends are life-saving medicine.

ECCLESIASTICUS 6:14–16

SEPTEMBER

Adaptation of Psalm 1

Blessed is the one who does not blend in with wrongdoers or sit quietly when they gossip or mock. Blessed is the one who tries to be a Christian and thinks deeply about how to follow it through. That person is like a tree planted by streams of water, which yields its fruit in season, sometimes gets knocked by wind but is growing and makes a difference.

> *Happy are those*
> *   who do not follow the advice of the wicked,*
> *or take the path that sinners tread,*
> *   or sit in the seat of scoffers;*
> *but their delight is in the law of the Lord,*
> *   and on his law they meditate day and night.*
> *They are like trees*
> *   planted by streams of water,*
> *which yield their fruit in its season,*
> *   and their leaves do not wither.*
> *In all that they do, they prosper.*
>
> PSALM 1:1–3

14

SEPTEMBER

A Wellness Check as You Return to School

Dear Lord,

Guide me …

- To check what is being asked of me and know what I can do.
- To commit to things and see them through.
- To prioritise my time and pursue a hobby.
- To develop a good routine as I prepare for sleep.
- To be aware of how food and exercise affect how I feel.

Guide me …

- To create more fun and to think positively.
- To devise a relaxation plan and learn that to say NO is sometimes okay.
- To have something to look forward to and make work part of my life, not all of it.
- To take regular mini-breaks and cultivate confidence so that I can be the best that I can be.

Amen.

You who live in the shelter of the Most High,
who abide in the shadow of the Almighty,
will say to the Lord, 'My refuge and my fortress;
my God, in whom I trust.'

PSALM 91:1–2

OCTOBER

Mission Month: Head, Heart and Hand

October is Mission Month. For our school, in so many of our school subjects and as part of our mission as Christians, we pay attention to justice issues in the world.

It is important to connect the
- head (what we understand),
- heart (what we feel)
- and hand (what we can do),

so that our work is useful and meaningful.

Dear Lord,
as students of the world, we are learning to read the world
and engage critically.
We know we are called to help those on the margins,
just as Jesus did ...
Personally .... through our actions
Locally .... in our community
Nationally .... supporting campaigns
Internationally................................ responding to poverty
Globally .... caring for our common home
We ask your guidance to respond to this call, through Christ our Lord.
Amen.

OCTOBER

Mission Month:
Make Friends with the Unlikely

The call is to reach out to those who would be unlikely friends. When someone has done wrong, they may already feel vulnerable. Could you be the one to show care and not add to their pain, exploitation or isolation? Could you help someone else not to hold a grudge? Could you pray for a thief, a bully or a prisoner? It is easy to care for nice people. Can we care for those who hurt others?

When Jesus perceived their questionings, he answered them, 'Why do you raise such questions in your hearts? Which is easier, to say, "Your sins are forgiven you", or to say, "Stand up and walk"? But so that you may know that the Son of Man has authority on earth to forgive sins' – he said to the one who was paralysed – 'I say to you, stand up and take your bed and go to your home.'

LUKE 5:22–24

OCTOBER

Mission Month: The Marginalised

Some people live in the poor world, some people live in the rich
Some people need food and water and haven't even a stitch

Some of us travel to Disneyland to treat ourselves to fun
More of us travel for water because more of us have none

Everyone is hungry for something or other in life
Your mental health might suffer or you may live by a knife

Some fight for their own lives while others turn away
And we learn to donate and feel better while we tell them that they cannot stay

They are different from me and I am not right about it all
Colour, religion, culture, the world is in fact quite small

I don't own this earth; I share it with you and them
So tomorrow let's open the stable, like the story from way back when.

Dear Lord,
help us to:
work to dispel stereotypes about the world's marginalised,
be active in society adovacting for fair economic systems,
speak about the alternative to systems that keep people in vulnerable
situations.
We ask this through Christ Our Lord. Amen.

OCTOBER

Mid-term Break

At mid-term we are grateful for times of rest.

Lord, we thank you for this time of rest and reflection from the busy-ness of life.

Thank you for these moments.

May we be able to give comfort and rest to others, to spread calmness, not chaos.

During the coming days take our burdens and replace them with calm.

During the coming days help us to rest from the unending work, so that any work we do will be productive.

During the coming days give us comfort so that we can find new strength, new wisdom, new power.

Touch the lives and hearts of those around us.

And, as we begin to work again, help us to feel renewed in your presence. Amen.

Therefore, while the promise of entering his rest is still open, let us take care that none of you should seem to have failed to reach it. For indeed the good news came to us just as to them; but the message they heard did not benefit them, because they were not united by faith with those who listened. For in one place it speaks about the seventh day as follows: 'And God rested on the seventh day from all his works.'

HEBREWS 4:1–2, 4

OCTOBER

Giving Thanks

Today we focus on giving thanks.

We gather as a school community, giving thanks for the blessings we received during our first half term and to ask the Lord's continuing blessing on this new school year.

It has been a time of renewed energies and eager anticipation.

It has been a time of acknowledgement of the challenges ahead.

We give thanks for all our new pupils and staff.

We pray today for ourselves and for each other, that we may support and help each other in the months ahead.

Lord God, you are always with us. Help us as we continue this year together.

May we use the gifts you have given us during the coming months and so continue to grow to our full potential.

We make our prayer through Christ our Lord. Amen.

But we appeal to you, brothers and sisters, to respect those who labour among you, and have charge of you in the Lord and admonish you; esteem them very highly in love because of their work. Be at peace among yourselves.

1 Thessalonians 5:12–13

OCTOBER

Be with Us Today, Lord

Dear Lord,
may all we do today, begin with you.
Plant dreams and hopes, which revive any tired spirits.
Be with us today.
May all we do today, be supported by you.
Be at our side, so that glimpses of you are present
in people we meet and places we pause in.
Be our support today.
May all we do today, lead to tomorrow;
our efforts, our work, being part of a journey
on paths that are rich to be on right now
but also lead to brightness ahead.
Let your presence go beyond today. Amen.

A Prayer for Grace
Gracious God,
fill the world with the consolation of your love so that each and all may
know that daily and simple actions of kindness
and love change our world.
Show us how we can share your grace and life and be good news
to those with whom we live and work. Amen.

NOVEMBER

A Farmer's Reflection

They do not speak to me, the animals,
unless, of course, I listen.
I work the land, the farm, the animals, the food and milk,
the grass, the soil, the tractor.
Bless all farmers:
the strength in their bodies that brings food to our plates,
the strength of them, as they arise to greet the sun and the animals.
Lord, look on them with kindness,
as they give more than they feel they can.
They provide for their families, their communities,
they love the earth as they give back.
Lord, renew.
As light changes each morning, we awaken to the light and the invitation to
a new day in the world.
Each night, we surrender to the dark, to be taken, to relax, to rest, to pray.
Amen.

Love righteousness, you rulers of the earth,
think of the Lord in goodness
and seek him with sincerity of heart.

WISDOM 1:1

NOVEMBER

In Thanks for the Harvest

Today, we give thanks for the Harvest, for all the fruits of the Earth.

Dear Lord,
we ask your blessings on the produce of the harvest.
We are thankful for what is plentiful in farms and gardens,
in shops and supermarkets, what is plentiful in our homes.
You fill our lives with abundance, variety and colour.
Thank you for the inner harvest of the heart.
Help us to cherish and respect the earth,
to share our bread with the hungry,
to treasure and appreciate what we have been given.
We make this prayer through Christ our Lord.
Amen.

*And God said, 'Let there be lights in the dome of the sky to separate
the day from the night; and let them be for signs and for seasons and
for days and years, and let them be lights in the dome of the sky to
give light upon the earth.' And it was so.*

GENESIS 1:14–15

NOVEMBER

Finding Comfort When There Is Loss

In death, we find the good in people, in the person who has died, in those who loved them, in those who come to envelop us, to support our pain and our loss.

We find good because we find perspective. Those moments and misdemeanours are only part of the day, of that day, and they leave us, rightly, because they are not the total, they are only a part. The drive for power can provoke a great urge to be right, and in death God has the last word, so neither you nor I was right. But death is not the final word.

Dear Lord,
you raise me up, so I can stand on mountains,
so I can value the good, the beauty and the truth
and rejoice in all that is, as it is. Amen.

> *Love is patient; love is kind; love is not envious or boastful or arrogant or rude. It does not insist on its own way; it is not irritable or resentful; it does not rejoice in wrongdoing, but rejoices in the truth. It bears all things, believes all things, hopes all things, endures all things. Love never ends.*

> 1 CORINTHIANS 13: 4–8

NOVEMBER

For the Holy Souls

Lord,
today we thank you for all the people who have gone before us.
We thank you for all that we have inherited and learned from them.
We have recalled those we have known
but we realise that there are many we know nothing of
and yet we share their genes and inherit their gifts.
Help us in our lives to be true to their memory.
Gather these holy souls into your kingdom
of happiness and peace. Amen.

St Paul teaches that prayer must involve both the spirit and the mind:

> *For if I pray in a tongue, my spirit prays but my mind is unproductive. What should I do then? I will pray with the spirit, but I will pray with the mind also; I will sing praise with the spirit, but I will sing praise with the mind also.*
>
> 1 CORINTHIANS 14:14–15

> *It is the same way with lifeless instruments that produce sound, such as the flute or the harp. If they do not give distinct notes, how will anyone know what is being played?*
>
> 1 CORINTHIANS 14:7

NOVEMBER

God Didn't Make Death

God takes no delight in the ruin of anything that lives.
God created everything so that it might exist.
The creative forces at work in the cosmos are life-giving.
There is no destructive poison in them.
The underworld doesn't rule on earth.
Doing what is right means living forever.

Dear Lord,
surround us with your care.
Be with us in grief, when things feel unsure.
And give us strength and reasons to hope.
Wrap those who have died in peace!
And give them rest.
We give them to you.
We remember all our loved ones
who have died,
and we pray for them in this holy month of November.
Amen.

*Take, Lord, and receive all my liberty, my memory, my understanding,
and my entire will, all I have and call my own. You have given all
to me. To you, Lord, I return it. Everything is yours; do with it what
you will. Give me only your love and your grace, that is enough for
me.*

St Ignatius of Loyola

DECEMBER

Advent: A Time of Waiting

The season of Advent sometimes seems lost in the consumerist jump from Halloween to Christmas. Ghostly ghouls are replaced with sparkling lights and there is no pause, no waiting in between. All is now, all is here.

A consumer culture teaches us that we should never have to wait, but that anything can be had at any time.

- Advent is a time of preparation and waiting. Slow down.
- Advent is a time to be present to ourselves, to notice God's presence among us.
- Advent is a time of sharing and caring and practising the kindness that we emphasise at Christmas.

Resist the rush. This Advent, be aware, prepare, notice what is there.

Our Prayer This Advent
Dear Lord,
give us the grace to live with the things
that don't balance out as we would like,
an acceptance of the blessings that have come our way.
The graces of wisdom and insight
are evident in the stories of Advent and Christmas. Amen.

DECEMBER

Advent Wreath

We gather around this Advent wreath to celebrate the beginning of the holy season of Advent. The word *advent* means 'coming'. We join with the Church throughout the world to prepare for the coming of Jesus Christ.

We light the first purple candle. It represents the virtue of love. Jesus loves us so much that he became human to be our Saviour, to teach us to follow him. Jesus has told us that the greatest commandment is to love God with all our hearts, souls and minds.

We look forward to the Advent themes of LOVE, FAITH, JOY, HOPE.

> *Open the gates,*
> *so that the righteous nation that keeps faith*
> *may enter in.*
> *Those of steadfast mind you keep in peace –*
> *in peace because they trust in you.*
> *Trust in the Lord for ever,*
> *for in the Lord God*
> *you have an everlasting rock.*
>
> ISAIAH 26:2–4

DECEMBER

Is Christmas for Holy People? Are You Holy?

People don't seem to want to be seen to be holy or call themselves holy. We don't say we are religious. It seems negative. We say 'I am spiritual'.
It is hard to be holy. 'Holy' means connected to God. So, respond to the part of your being that feels connected to God. If you don't go to Mass then pray somewhere else. If you don't pray then close your eyes and reflect. If you are more of a do-er then act as Jesus would. Be kind, loving and supportive. And start with yourself. Be holy. Be careful, you might miss Jesus in the crowd.

A Priest You Know
When you look at a priest you know, do you ever wonder if he feels under pressure about what he might say at Mass? Striving to prepare to speak at Christmas is a real challenge. There will be people in the church who don't normally go to Mass. When Jesus sent out the Twelve, he knew they were needed. Do our priests feel needed? Not just in the sacraments, but in their very presence as priests amongst us? Take time to acknowledge, thank and pray for a priest you know.

A Prayer for Clergy
Dear Lord,
bless our clergy,
guide their words,
comfort them as they comfort others.
Lay your hands on their holy hands, in every sacrament and blessing.
Amen.

DECEMBER

Christmas Carols

Christmas music is everywhere but don't forget the carols. The story of the carols is intense. Where are Mary and Joseph at this part of the Christmas story?

Herod has called a census. Mary and Joseph are on the move in exhausting conditions, an echo of refugees today who are on the move or waiting in exhausting conditions. While we are looking forward to something good, a Christmas celebration, refugees do not know how things will end or turn out. Will their lives turn into celebration?

Be generous this Advent. Can you give to refugees, pray for them or lobby on their behalf? Can you create positivity where there is racism and injustice? The Wise Kings brought gifts, so the story of the carols repeats itself year after year.

Let us go to Bethlehem and see what has occurred.

In that region there were shepherds living in the fields, keeping watch over their flock by night. Then an angel of the Lord stood before them, and the glory of the Lord shone around them, and they were terrified. But the angel said to them, 'Do not be afraid; for see – I am bringing you good news of great joy for all the people: to you is born this day in the city of David a Saviour, who is the Messiah, the Lord. This will be a sign for you: you will find a child wrapped in bands of cloth and lying in a manger.' And suddenly there was with the angel a multitude of the heavenly host, praising God and saying,
    Glory to God in the highest heaven,
    and on earth peace among those whom he favours!'
When the angels had left them and gone into heaven, the shepherds said to one another, 'Let us go now to Bethlehem and see this thing that has taken place, which the Lord has made known to us.' So they went with haste and found Mary and Joseph, and the child lying in the manger. When they saw this, they made known what had been told them about this child; and all who heard it were amazed at what the shepherds told them. But Mary treasured all these words and pondered them in her heart. The shepherds returned, glorifying and praising God for all they had heard and seen, as it had been told them.

LUKE 2:8–20

DECEMBER

Advent, the Pink Candle: for Joy

What brings you joy?
A beautiful book, a chat with a friend, a YouTube clip shared, a child you know, an older person you know?
Dancing, food, a piece of music, relaxing, sleep, dressing up, doing your hair?
A quiet house, a noisy house, a cup of tea?
The joy of success, exam results, knowing you helped someone?
Laughing, sport, the adrenalin of exercise?
The birds singing, warmth, a familiar smell, the joy of joy?

May God be gracious to us and bless us
and make his face to shine upon us,
Selah
that your way may be known upon earth,
your saving power among all nations.
Let the peoples praise you, O God;
let all the peoples praise you.

Let the nations be glad and sing for joy,
for you judge the peoples with equity
and guide the nations upon earth.
Selah
Let the peoples praise you, O God;
let all the peoples praise you.

PSALM 67:1–5

JANUARY

A New Year: Begin Again

Dear Lord,

we gather today as a community, together again, giving thanks for the blessings we received during our Christmas holidays and to ask the Lord's continuing blessing on our school year.

The candle-lighting represents Christ amongst us and it joins this year to last year.

We pray today for ourselves and each other, that we may support and help each other in the months ahead. Lord, you are always with us. May we use the gifts you have given us during the coming months and so continue to work to our full potential. Amen.

Prayers of the Faithful

1. We pray for the students, that they may work hard and enjoy their days here in school. That those who feel most under pressure find support amongst us.

Lord, hear us. Lord, graciously hear us.

2. We pray for all staff, that we may take note of the students' achievements and encourage them. That we may be guided in our teaching and learning.

Lord, hear us. Lord, graciously hear us.

3. We pray for retired staff and past pupils. That they, who have built

our foundations, are enjoying happiness in new stages of their lives.
Lord, hear us. Lord, graciously hear us.

4. We pray for the sick. We remember staff and students who are touched by illness during the school year. That school may be a place of friendship and support and prayer for their intentions.
Lord, hear us. Lord, graciously hear us.

Amen.

JANUARY

Beatitudes for the Adolescent

Creating a mood of thanksgiving.

Happy are the quiet, for they will enjoy all things.

Happy are the reflective, for they will experience God's mercy.

Happy are the sensitive, for they will be in tune with society.

Happy are those who seek justice, for they will be rewarded.

Happy are those who forgive, for they will be forgiven.

Happy are those who are selfless, for they will be praised.

Happy are the peacemakers, for they are examples to us all.

Happy are those who stand up for others, for they will have light in their lives.

WRITTEN BY FIFTH-YEAR STUDENTS, CRESCENT COLLEGE
COMPREHENSIVE SJ 2016. FOR CATHOLIC SCHOOLS WEEK

Dear Lord,

thank you for another new year and for new chances every day. We pray for peace, for light and for hope, that we might spread them to others.

We accept your gift of a new year and we rejoice in what's ahead, depending on you to help us do exactly what you want. Amen.

'Blessed are the poor in spirit, for theirs is the kingdom of heaven.

'Blessed are those who mourn, for they will be comforted.

'Blessed are the meek, for they will inherit the earth.

'Blessed are those who hunger and thirst for righteousness, for they will be filled.

'Blessed are the merciful, for they will receive mercy.

'Blessed are the pure in heart, for they will see God.

'Blessed are the peacemakers, for they will be called children of God.

'Blessed are those who are persecuted for righteousness' sake, for theirs is the kingdom of heaven.'

MATTHEW 5:3–10

JANUARY

Catholic Schools Week: Hope

Let us make a special effort to spread good energies throughout our school during Catholic Schools Week.

Hope brings all sorts of other good energies with it: optimism, positivity, enthusiasm, courage, resilience, motivation. It is the gift that keeps on giving. And we can give that gift to others in our school. We can 'work on' hope, develop it, pray for it, spread it and show it in the way we relate to others. It can be a light to show us the way, the energy to keep that light burning brightly, a vehicle to carry us on our way, a pit stop where we can refresh. It does not demand repayment.

The poet Emily Dickinson wrote of hope:
> 'never, in extremity / it asked a thing of me'

You may not always have a comfortable life and you will not always be able to solve all of the world's problems at once but don't ever underestimate the importance you can have because history has shown us that courage can be contagious and hope can take on a life of its own.

MICHELLE OBAMA

FEBRUARY

St Brigid's Day

As February begins, we take note of it as the month of healing.
We remember the healing influence of St Brigid, whose feast day is on the
first of February.

We bring our prayers before the Lord.

Dear Lord,
you called St Brigid to teach the new commandment of love, through
her life of hospitality and her care of those in need.
Give to your people a generous spirit,
so that, with hearts made pure,
we may show your love to all. Amen.

> *I wait for the Lord, my soul waits,*
> *and in his word I hope.*
>
> PSALM 130:5

FEBRUARY

A Month of Healing

In February, nature is healed from the winter harshness.

Healing can be found in the friendship and support of the community gathered here this morning.

As springtime begins, we pray for new beginnings, especially as we try to change old habits. We look at our school and environment and consider how can we improve it to make it a better place to be.

The Lord is my shepherd, I shall not want.
He makes me lie down in green pastures;
he leads me beside still waters;
he restores my soul.
He leads me in right paths
for his name's sake.

Even though I walk through the darkest valley,
I fear no evil;
for you are with me;
your rod and your staff –
they comfort me.

You prepare a table before me
in the presence of my enemies;
you anoint my head with oil;
my cup overflows.
Surely goodness and mercy shall follow me
all the days of my life,
and I shall dwell in the house of the Lord
my whole life long.

PSALM 23

FEBRUARY

Springtime Contemplation

We look at our school and environment and consider how can we improve it to make it a better place to be.

Spring is a good time to make new beginnings in your own life.
- What is growing in the warmth of your soul?
- Where are there signs of decay?
- What is being raised to new life within you?
- What is bursting into new growth?

Dear Lord,
give to your people a generous spirit,
so that, with hearts made pure,
we may show your love to all. Amen.

There a blanket of crispy and crunchy leaves beneath each bare tree.
Trees patiently waiting to be wrapped in leaves just in time for,
birds creating homes, insects emerging from hibernation, a birth of
a new generation.

IONA LOGAN, CLASS OF 2021

FEBRUARY

Valentine's Day

Valentine's Day is a great day to give thanks for those we love, for any reason.

May your life be filled with the blessings of love.
May the spiritual bond that unites you
with your loved ones draw you closer.
When you are together, may your lives be enriched.
May you be connected, mind, heart and soul.
And may God bless your thoughts and feelings for those
you love in all ways. Amen.

> *Love is patient; love is kind; love is not envious or boastful or*
> *arrogant or rude. It does not insist on its own way; it is not irritable*
> *or resentful; it does not rejoice in wrongdoing, but rejoices in the*
> *truth. It bears all things, believes all things, hopes all things, endures*
> *all things.*
> *Love never ends.*
>
> 1 Corinthians 13:4–7

FEBRUARY

Christian Unity

If you never read Scripture, take these words with you today:
Blessed are you.

Lord, I welcome this day to celebrate Christians. All Christians.
It is your gift to me,
the first day of the rest of our lives.
I thank you for the gift of being alive, this morning.
I thank you for the sleep which has refreshed me.
I thank you for the chance to start things all over again.
Lord, this day is full of promise and opportunity.
Guide me to waste none of it.
This day is full of mystery and unknown at this moment:
help me to face it without anxiety.
During this day, may I become
a more thoughtful person,
a more prayerful person,
a more generous and kinder person.
Bless this day for us all in a spirit of Christian harmony. Amen.

So if anyone is in Christ,
there is a new creation:
everything old has passed away;
look, new things have come into being.

2 CORINTHIANS 5: 17

MARCH

Seachtain na Gaeilge

To mark Seachtain na Gaeilge, a week celebrating all things Irish, we pray today an Irish blessing:

Go raibh beannachtai an tsolais ort ar an taobh istigh
agus ar an taobh amuigh,
Go bhfásfadh do chroí le teas cosúil le tine
Ag fáiltiú roimh chairde agus strainséirí araon.
Go mbeannódh neart na gaoithe tú
Go n-iompródh an bháisteach chun spriod a ghlanadh
Go raibh beannachtaí Dé ort
Ionas go mbeadh focal cineálta agat dóibh siúd a mbuaileann tú leo.
Go Dtuige tú go bhfuil pairt tabhabhtach
Agat I bpleananna Dé.
Is féidir leat tuiscint a fháil ar neart Dé agus cumhach
Go dtuige tú neart agus cumhacht Dé
Agus ciúineas síoraí na ndúl. Amen.

May the blessing of light be upon you
On the inside, on the outside,
Your heart grows with warmth like a fire
Welcoming friends and strangers alike
The strengths of the winds bless you

Carrying the rain to wash your spirit clean
The blessings of God's earth be on you
So that you have a kind word for those you meet.
May you realise that in this great universe,
You are a part of God's plan.
May you understand God's strength and power
And the quiet beauty of creation. Amen.

MARCH

Lent: Lenten Promises

Sometimes when we give up things for Lent, it is more to do with personal health than Christian witness.

Being a Christian means performing acts of kindness.

It is speaking out what has to be said, despite being afraid.

It is standing up for yourself, despite feeling you're a nobody.

It is overcoming apathy and committing to making an effort.

It is staying with someone who is downhearted.

It is choosing to side with people who are unfairly treated.

It is getting involved in community and working hard.

We must journey with hope and courage into the future.

JIM MAHER SJ

Lenten Prayer
God of all that is good,
we thank you for what we have been given, and we kindly ask you for the generosity and kindness to use well what we have recieved from our families, our friends and our school.

When things don't work out as we would like, we are confident that you are teaching us life lessons that will stay with us about what's most important: health, family, friendship, community, being boys and girls, men and women generously reaching out to others.

We pray for those who are lonely and have to cope on their own. When Lent begins, we ask you to guide us in the right direction during those forty days, so that we may continue to grow into the people of kindness and friendship that you want us to be. Amen.

JIM MAHER SJ

MARCH

In Thanks for Food and Water

As the holy season of Lent continues, we remind ourselves of this time of prayer in preparation for Easter.

- When we think of the nearness of God at Easter we should trust in his goodness.
- When we know the truth of his story, we will recognise his presence in others.
- If the mystery is hard to understand, we could take quiet time in prayer.
- If we are unsure about choices, one word can come and encourage us.

A Prayerful Pause, in Thanks for Food

Remember the Grace before Meals?

Take a moment before you eat to thank God for food.

Be thankful for the company you are in.

Appreciate the food before you.

Give thanks for the way the food will nourish your body and prepare you for the next part of your day.

Share meals with family as a means of helping relationships to grow.

Share treats with others to create a smile.

Never waste food: it is a precious resource.

A Prayerful Pause, in Thanks for Water

Living water.

Come, all who are thirsty,

dip your hands in the stream,

refresh body and mind.

Drink from it, depend on it, for this water will never run dry.

Come, all who are thirsty, says Jesus, our Lord.

MARCH

St Patrick's Day

As we gather, we celebrate, value and treasure all that is good about Ireland and about Irish people.

We join with the whole world in celebrating the contribution Irish people have made, and continue to make, to our world. We remember those who had to leave home because of poverty, famine and lack of employment.

We focus on our flag: it's a sign of our identity, belonging and unity. May its bright colours of green, white and gold lift our hearts, give us hope and keep us one.

Unite, protect and strengthen your Church throughout the world. Sustain N., our Pope. Guide our leaders in faith. Be close to all God's faithful people. Together may we witness to true gospel living in our daily lives.

Lord, we are thankful for:

- the gift of courage which Patrick showed in returning to Ireland and facing many dangers in his work of spreading the Christian message.
- the gift of prayer in good times and in bad.
- the ability to listen to the voice of God speaking in our hearts.
- Irish people all over the world – those who have been successful and content and those whose dreams have not been fulfilled.
- all who have chosen to make Ireland their home. May they feel welcome among us and succeed in building the lives of their dreams. Amen.

St Patrick's Breastplate

I arise today, through a mighty strength:
God's power to guide me,
God's might to uphold me,
God's eyes to watch over me; God's ear to hear me,
God's word to give me speech,
God's hand to guard me,
God's way to lie before me,
God's shield to shelter me,
God's host to secure me. Amen.

APRIL

Lenten Reflection

As the holy season of Lent continues we remind ourselves of this time of prayer in preparation for Easter.

- When we think of the nearness of God at Easter we should trust in his goodness.
- When we know the truth of his story, we will recognise his presence in others.
- If the mystery is hard to understand, we could take quiet time in prayer.
- If we are unsure about choices, one word can come and encourage us.

Lord, listen to the prayers of the community as we gather,
that we will give and receive,
that we will serve and reach out,
so, that relationships and hospitality, forgiveness and fairness become actions of our faith. Amen.

APRIL

Holy Week with Prayers of the Faithful

Holy Week is the high point of the Church's calendar.

As we enter Holy Week, we ask you to watch out for, and reach out to, those who are lonely or troubled. Renew your Lenten promises and make time for reflection and prayer. Your local parishes will have many ceremonies remembering the events of Holy Week.

It is a special time to ask the question as they did at the empty tomb: Where is Jesus?

'Who do people say that the Son of Man is?' And they said, 'Some say John the Baptist, but others Elijah, and still others Jeremiah or one of the prophets.' He said to them, 'But who do you say that I am?' Simon Peter answered, 'You are the Messiah, the Son of the living God.' And Jesus answered him, 'Blessed are you, Simon son of Jonah! For flesh and blood has not revealed this to you, but my Father in heaven. And I tell you, you are Peter, and on this rock I will build my church.'

MATTHEW 16:13–18

Come Holy Spirit, fill me up
And reign in me this day
So that everything I think, and say and do
Will be inspired by you.
God our Father
By your Spirit at work in me
May I seek and find you in all things this day,
And by your Grace, may others seek and find something of you in
me.
Amen.

ANN GUINEE

The message of Easter is one of hope.
Deep within ourselves we carry hope.
If not, there is no hope.
Hope is a quality of the soul
and does not depend on what's happening in the world.
Hope is not about predicting the future.
It is a direction of the spirit,
a direction of the heart,
anchored beyond the horizon.

Dear Lord,
help us keep in mind that Christ lives with you in glory
and has promised to remain with us until the end of time.
When we encounter suffering give us the strength to act on our compassion.
Help us to spread the joy of your resurrection.
Amen.

Prayers of the Faithful

1. We pray for the leaders of the Catholic Church, for N., our Pope, for N., our bishop.

May the Spirit guide their work.

Lord, hear us.

Lord, graciously hear us.

2. We pray for the leaders of our country, that they will be honest, hardworking and cautious in their decision-making.

We pray that they will respond to the plight of the homeless, the sick and those in need.

We pray that they will respond to the call to be global citizens responsible for the care of the planet and those in it.

Lord, hear us.

Lord, graciously hear us.

3. We pray for the sick.

We acknowledge those in our school and its wider community who are challenged by their physical or mental health.

Our prayer is that they will find support in their friends and families and compassion in those who care for them.

Lord, hear us.

Lord, graciously hear us.

4. We pray for the school community, for all who work to make our school a place

where we strive to do our best;

where social justice is awakened;

where caring for the individual is at the heart of all our interactions.

We pray for the sixth and third years sitting exams at this time. Bless all our efforts.

Lord, hear us.

Lord, graciously hear us.

5. We pray for courage as we make our Lenten promises:
that we are inspired today to be brave enough to challenge ourselves;
that each time we remember that we are giving up something for Lent that we
engage it with our faith and say a prayer for another.

Lord, hear us.
Lord, graciously hear us.

6. We pray for our loved ones who have passed away:
for those whom we have known and loved and who are now in the hands of
the Lord;
for young and old, those who have had an untimely or sudden passing.
We remember also, those who are part of our school's list of the deceased.
May they rest in peace.

Lord, hear us.
Lord, graciously hear us..

We make all our prayers through Christ Our Lord. Amen.

APRIL

On the Day of a Match

We focus on sport today as we have an important match.
When we pray in sport, should we pray to win?
Well, it depends on whose team you think God is on!
Sport is good for all: players, coaches and supporters. It gives us a reason to bond together and show each other Christian qualities.
When we win, we could all enjoy some little bit of it. When we don't win, we show another type of support, equally important.
We are thankful that we have sport in our school, we are especially thankful to the players, for their hard work and dedication. We are also thankful for the way the school shares the joy.

Today is game day, so what do we pray for?

Help us to be committed sports people who play for the good of our team. Help us to find the strength to bring all our skills, work and dedication to the fore.

Lord, you have surrounded us with people who always look out for us. You have given us a family in school who bless us every day with kind words and actions. They lift us up in ways that keep our eyes focused on you, so we find God in all things.

We are grateful for sporting success but also for the gifts it allows us to share and display. Amen.

APRIL

Slow to the Beat

Slow, slow, quick, quick, slow ... ...
Familiar words of a learner dancer, talking to themselves the beat of the
music.
Dance to your own beat.
Breathe in time with life, set the pace and reassure your mind that you are in
control.
Bring the mind, body and soul to your own beat.
Breathe in 2 ... 3 ... 4, breathe out 2 ... 3 ... 4, and in 2 ... 3 ...

Send the oxygen on its journey around your body, travelling in your blood
through your veins,
telling all in its path that the beat has changed.
It is slow, slow, calm and slow.

Dear Lord,
help us keep in mind that Christ lives with you in glory and has
promised to remain with us until the end of time. When we encounter
suffering give us the strength to act on our compassion. Help us to
spread the joy of your resurrection. Amen.

MAY

Exam Preparations

We give thanks for the year gone by, for the work done and for those who led us in doing it.

We pray for those preparing for the Junior and Leaving Cert in June and those doing house exams.

Lord, calm our fears at exam time.

Let the work we have done stand to us on the day.

Do not allow what remains undone to undermine our courage.

Help us to make the best of our knowledge.

Exams are only part of what is going on in our lives at the moment.

Bless our families and friends at this time too.

Guide us as we prepare further for exams and keep us from getting disheartened and over-worried.

Lead us in safety through the weeks ahead.

We make this prayer through Christ Our Lord. Amen.

Exam Prayer

Dear Lord,

we give thanks for the new start we have made, for the work done and for those who led us in doing it.

We pray for those receiving exam results today and admire the support they give to each other.

We remember those who find work challenging in any way.

We have been blessed with various talents. Help us to have the courage to use them to the best of our abilities.

Lead us all in safety through the weeks ahead.

We make this prayer through Christ Our Lord. Amen.

MAY

Our Lady

Our Lady, we turn to you as Mother of Jesus and Leader of all.
Knowing the decisions you made in your life, we ask you to join us as we make our decisions.
Every day our decisions make a difference, small or big.
We pray for peace of mind in decision-making so that the options are real and the pathways are varied. Help us to know that there are times to pause, times that are not right to make decisions. We need to be settled; we need calmness. Above all guide our decision-making and help us to know that, as we journey, one decision leads to another.

Sé do bheath' a Mhuire,
atá lán de ghrásta, tá an Tiarna leat.
Is beannaithe thú idir mná
agus is beannaithe toradh do bhruinne Iosa.
A Naomh Mhuire, a mháthair Dé,
guí orainn na peacaithe, anois is ar uair ar mbás. Amen.

MAY

Prayer in the Muslim Tradition

In this Holy Month of Ramadan, a reading from the Quran, in English.

In the name of God, the most gracious, the most Merciful
All praise and thanks are God's,
the Lord of mankind and all that exists,
the most gracious, the most Merciful,
the only Owner and the only ruling judge.
The day of Recompense, that is the day of Resurrection.
You alone we worship,
and you alone we ask for help for each and every thing.
Guide us to the straight way by those on whom
you bestowed your Grace,
not of those who earned your anger,
not of those who went astray. Amen.

MAY

In Thanks for the Experience
of Transition Year

St Ignatius is known to have struggled with studying at stages in his life. He was not a typical, run-of-the-mill student, but when he got serious about his study he could not be distracted.

As we leave Transition Year, we reflect on the question: are you aware of any gifts in you that can transform your environment and those in it? St Ignatius taught his Jesuit students that they should appreciate academic learning and degrees in the world in which they lived. But there was something about the spell of his personality that gave him a certain command over his fellow students.

So, as we return to a more academic focus in school, and having explored our way through Transition Year, we pray that we use the gifts and talents that we have given time to discover and enjoy in the next stage of our time at school.

Prayer for My Fellow Students
May you discover enough goodness in others to believe in a world of peace. May a kind word, a reassuring touch, a warm smile be yours every day, and may you give these gifts as well as
you have received them.
Teach love to others, and let that love embrace you,
so that you may call upon them.
Lord, help us to make the best of our skills.
You have a loving plan for our lives.
Guide us in gratitude for Transition Year.
Help us to relish the opportunity to enjoy a refreshing break. Amen.

MAY

The Examen

Let's sit down and watch the video of our year, with gratitude.
When you say thanks, you give yourself the gift of positivity.
Thanks is like food for the heart and soul and gives us confidence.
When you thank a person, they pay attention to the kindness they gave, in case they had not seen it before.
Be thankful for a compliment,
for help with study,
for a listening ear,
for conversations, for friendship, for fun.
This building is full of memories of your year.

When we are grateful, we are positive.
We notice what is good at that moment.

The Daily Examen
1. Become aware of God's presence.
   Be still, be quiet, relax.
2. Look back over today with gratitude.
   Look back over your day and notice what was good.
3. What was difficult about today?
   What can you do about that?
   Are you part of the answer?
4. Discern:
   pause and see what else comes to mind.
5. Look forward to the day ahead.
   What can you do to make it good?

Say the Our Father or the Prayer of St Ignatius.

Prayer of St Ignatius

Dearest Lord,

teach me to be generous;

to serve you as you deserve to be served;

to give and not to count the cost,

to fight and not to heed the wounds,

to toil and not to seek for rest,

to labour and not to ask for reward

save that of knowing I do your most holy will. Amen.

JUNE

God Has a Plan for You

It is by trusting in God's plan that we find comfort.
In Jeremiah, we find well-known words which people leaving school always like:
'I know the plans I have for you.' (Jeremiah 29:11)
As the year draws to a close try to trust that God is part of your plan, that you are part of God's plan.

Above all trust in the slow work of God.
We are naturally impatient in everything,
to reach the end without delay
We should like to skip the intermediate stages.
We are impatient of being on the way to something unknown,
something new.
And yet it is the law of all progress
that it is made by passing through some stages of instability –
and that it may take a very long time.

PIERRE TEILHARD DE CHARDIN SJ

JULY

Past Pupils

Past pupils leave a mark on their school.
They leave a mark on the people they meet.
They leave a mark on the staff and affirm them in their work.
It is because of past pupils that staff continue great traditions,
knowing that they are doing the right thing.

Past pupils have changed our school –
led us in different directions,
showed us the importance of our growth and change.
Their ambition refreshes us, their success enlivens us.
Their difficulties call us together, to say, 'We know!'

As pupils become past pupils, they should leave their school with
delight –
embrace the new!
Celebrate the natural change.
Take on the joys and challenges of the next stage
and encounter society as men and women for others.

AUGUST

An Adaptation of
Pope Francis's Message in Laudato Si'

Dear everyone in the world,
the Earth is God's gift to us and the fruits of the Earth belong to all.
The Earth has been mistreated by us. It does not have endless resources.
We have stripped the earth of some of its natural forests, contaminated
the waters, land and air.
Plants and species are becoming extinct.
Overuse of coal, oil and gas is helping to drive climate change.
Our common home is under threat and the poorest countries suffer.
Examine your lifestyles and check if you waste things and buy things you
don't need.
Our digital world can also mean that we don't live wisely, think deeply
and love generously.

PRAYERS AND REFLECTIONS FOR ANY TIME IN THE SCHOOL YEAR

Finding God in Nature

Life is not about what will happen
or what did happen.
It is about what is happening.
Look at the nature around you today. God is in it.
Creation is God's story.
'There is treasure in the fields,
there is treasure in the skies,
there is treasure in their meaning
from the Soul to the Eyes'.
So find God in nature, it will at least slow you down.
And who knows it may give you space to reflect on what will
happen and what did happen.

Board of Management

As we sit together, help us to put aside the other business of our day, the places and people we have come from and the things we need to do later. Help us to unite and focus on today's agenda. Each of us comes to this meeting with a valued perspective, our voices are important. We bring our experience and put what is best for the school community at the centre of our discussions, deliberations and decisions.

Dear Lord,
we pray for patience, listening, freedom and inspiration, and trust that your hand is in all we do. Amen.

When a Loved One is Sick

Dear Lord,

sit with me at this difficult time in my life.

Give me the courage I need to say and do what I need to.

Bless N., who is sick, and especially bless the hands that care for them in these days, so that they use their expertise and care at this challenging time. Give me courage to trust in you. Amen.

On Lighting a Candle

I light a candle
and suddenly the world around me changes;
one small flame is all it takes
to let the darkness know that it cannot win.

I Don't Want a Labrador

I don't want a Labrador,
2.4 kids don't appeal to me,
I'd rather have a chimpanzee.
A cockatoo, a kangaroo,
A trampoline, a mini zoo.
I don't want to work from 9–5,
Scraping pennies to stay alive.
Maybe I'll have a picket fence
Surrounding 4 big circus tents or
Maybe I'll swing from tree to tree
Shouting save the Eucalyptus please.

Who's to say what I'll be
Or what I'll meet or what I'll see.
But one thing I know for sure
I don't want a Labrador!

CAOIMH MCCARTHY, CLASS OF 2004

Prayer of St Ignatius

Dearest Lord,

teach me to be generous;

to serve you as you deserve to be served;

to give and not to count the cost,

to fight and not to heed the wounds,

to toil and not to seek for rest,

To labour and not to ask for reward

save that of knowing I do your most holy will. Amen.

A Special Introduction to the Examen

The Examen is a central prayer of St Ignatius and is familiar to those in Jesuit education as a way of stopping, tuning in to the movements of the day and continuing better equipped.

To quote a Jesuit teacher who uses the Examen: 'Things were going all wrong this morning, but I knew I could stop and start again.'

The Examen (of consciousness) involves an examination or intelligent paying attention to what is happening in our lives, with particular attention to the thoughts, feelings and desires behind our actions. It is not an examination of conscience. It is attending to what moves us deeply, to what especially strikes a chord. Beneath the surface of life, more is going on than we are conscious of. God speaks through our life experience, and by paying attention to the strong rumblings (positive and negative) we can come to know ourselves and God better, and to know what God wants to do to bring us the fullness of happiness and satisfaction. Like all things Ignatian there is no hard-and-fast way of doing this prayerful exercise. It can be adapted to suit personal circumstances. It takes 10–15 minutes, again depending on the circumstances.

A Version of the Five-Step Daily Examen that St Ignatius Practised

1. Become aware of God's presence, take this moment to settle
   yourself. Pause, breathe, step off the treadmill.
   Invite God.

2. Look back over your day so far, with gratitude. Take it step by step
   and recall what happened. Name what you are grateful for. Pay
   attention to the emotions that are emerging. Why am I feeling this?
   Is there a pattern to the experiences and feelings that follow? Can I
   recreate these?

3. Now take note of any negative moments. Arguments?
   Worries? Fears? Anxiety? Guilt? What conversations are playing on

your mind? What negative feelings are staying with you? Is there a pattern to this? Can you be part of the solution? Consider putting any difficult thoughts or feelings aside. Promise to come back to them later. Can you chat this through with someone later? Would it help to journal about it?

4. Pay attention to where you are now, start your day again with renewed energy. Give some space to see where your mind is leading you; give some space to see where God is leading you.

5. Look ahead now. Can you leave the first part of the day behind? Can you take learning from it? Slowly recite a prayer, poem or song you you know. Encourage yourself to continue with your day in a spirit of gratitude.